LANCASHIRE
STEAM FINALE

Nat 9/13.

45236

© Michael S Welch 2004

Published by Runpast Publishing, 10 Kingscote Grove, Cheltenham, Gloucestershire GL51 6JX.

ISBN 1 870754 61 1

Typesetting and reproduction by Viners Wood Associates. Printed in England by Clearpoint Colourprint Ltd.

Below: An enormously long freight train is wheeled through Garstang & Catterall station by Stanier Class 8F 2-8-0 No.48307 on 13th August 1965. This station was one of six intermediate stopping places between Preston and Lancaster and was located 9½ miles north of Preston, in a pleasantly rural part of Lancashire. It was closed from 3rd February 1969. Garstang & Catterall station survived for much longer than other wayside stations on this section of line. Barton & Broughton, Brock, Galgate and Scorton were very early closure victims and only lasted until 1st May 1939. Obviously, they could not have been money spinners for the LMSR! Bay Horse lasted longer and was open until 13th June 1960.   *Peter Fitton*

Introduction

When asked to describe the county of Lancashire in a single word, most ill-informed people from the south of England would almost certainly suggest 'dour', because to outsiders the county is the very embodiment of all that is conjured up by the dreaded words 'industrial north'. Quite apart from the fact that a soulless Hampshire town was recently voted as the dullest in Great Britain, this description would be a huge injustice to a county with a rich, arguably unsurpassed, industrial and cultural tradition. It is true that the rows of back-to-back terraced houses which typify some Lancashire towns could hardly be described as 'pretty', but at least these places have a real identity and character and have produced a wealth of really talented people, including world-renowned artists, comedians and musicians. Lancashire is, above all, a county of contrasts, those between the proud working class towns and the unashamed exuberance of Blackpool or the fashionable Lord Street shopping area in Southport could not be more marked.

To the railway aficionado, the county of Lancashire (which for the purposes of this volume includes Liverpool and Manchester) will always be remembered as the home of the world's first passenger-carrying railway: the line between Liverpool and Manchester opened with great ceremony on 15th September 1830. It would certainly be an understatement to say that rail transport came early to the county! Those involved in the construction of this railway had benefited greatly from the experiences of the early canal builders – the world's first canal was also in Lancashire – and when the line was being built many of the techniques used by the canal builders, such as tunnelling and building embankments, were already well developed. One of the greatest problems facing the mill and colliery owners of the day was the lack of adequate, reasonably quick, transport for their goods and the success of the Liverpool & Manchester Railway gave an immediate impetus to the building of other routes. Like railway lines in other parts of Great Britain these lines were largely promoted by groups of local people who wished to see their town connected to the rapidly expanding railway network. Most of these small concerns were soon absorbed by their mightier neighbours and the most prominent pre-grouping companies in Lancashire were, naturally, the Lancashire & Yorkshire Railway (LYR), plus the London & North Western Railway (LNWR). Another company that made an impact, despite its somewhat misleading name, was the Cheshire Lines Committee (CLC), this being one of the three companies which operated between Manchester and Liverpool by different routes.

A considerable proportion of the county's route mileage is situated between those cities, where a very dense and complex railway network was created as a result of the need to serve all of the major towns within the area and associated industrial installations. But Lancashire, as in many other respects, is a county of remarkable variety, and away from this belt of heavy industrial development there can be found some equally interesting and, in many cases, really attractive routes. One of the finest is the very scenic secondary line from Carnforth to Barrow-in-Furness, which offers some splendid vistas as it skirts the Lake District, and is well-known for some exceedingly long viaducts across wide river estuaries. Another distinctive line is the route from Blackburn to Hellifield, which traverses some beautiful rural countryside and gives worthwhile views of Pendle Hill, a landmark for miles around famous for its associations with witchcraft. It should be noted, however, that these lines were not wholly in Lancashire during the period covered by this album. The more recent history of the latter line is unusual because it lost its passenger trains in 1962, but remained open for freight traffic and occasional diverted through West Coast Main Line (WCML) passenger workings. Recently the local passenger service between Blackburn and Clitheroe was restored. The archetypal Lancashire towns of Bolton and Blackburn probably suffer from the unappealing industrial image as much as any, but the railway line between them passes through some stretches of quite lonely, wild moorland landscape. This is also one of the most steeply-graded lines in the county, climbing for many miles in each direction. The route from Wigan to Southport could not be more different, however, as this runs across a very fertile and extremely productive plain dotted with market gardens and smallholdings. Who said Lancashire was a county comprised solely of mill chimneys and collieries?

The decline in the fortunes of the railway industry was, mercifully, not felt quite as keenly in Lancashire as in many other parts of Great Britain, perhaps due to its very high population density and heavily used commuter lines around the large conurbations. Certainly, there were some early casualties, such as the Longridge to Preston and Knott End-on-Sea to Garstang & Catterall branches, both of which closed to passengers in 1930, while the Rochdale to Bacup line, which traversed a thinly populated rural area, lost its passenger trains in 1947. During the era of the Beeching cuts in the 1960s many lines in Lancashire were tabled for closure, but were reprieved, perhaps due to the circumstances mentioned above. One place that was unfortunate enough to lose its service was the sizeable industrial town of Leigh, while other losses included the Manchester to Accrington route, which boasted fearsome gradients over Baxenden summit, and the Windermere Lake Side branch, a line that had survived precariously for some years due to its heavy seasonal traffic. A particularly controversial closure was that of the link between Bolton and Rochdale via Bury, on the outskirts of Manchester.

In 1968 Lancashire became the final refuge of British Railways' standard gauge steam traction and because of this the county will always have a special place in the affections of steam enthusiasts up and down Great Britain, and even further afield. There cannot be many who do not cherish their memories of the indefinable, unique atmosphere at the last steam sheds of Carnforth, Lostock Hall and Rose Grove, an atmosphere that has, alas, proved almost impossible to recreate on preserved lines. The end of steam over Shap and the Settle & Carlisle routes at the end of 1967, and at Buxton in March 1968, meant that steam traction was confined to its final refuge in Lancashire, and hitherto anonymous long-distance freight workings from Wyre Dock to Healey Mills and suchlike suddenly gained a much higher profile. After trundling through Preston these workings took the East Lancashire line as far as Gannow Junction, Burnley, where they turned in a south-easterly direction and headed towards Todmorden. Besides being one of the most scenic routes remaining largely steam-worked during 1968, it was also one of the most steeply graded, the climbs often proving to be quite a challenge to engine crews working locomotives in indifferent condition, and very much on their 'last legs'. On the passenger side, steam's star turn was undoubtedly the 'Belfast Boat Express', a boat train which ran between Manchester Victoria and Heysham Harbour and vice versa. Incredibly, this train had been dieselised in the early 1960s using the unpredictable Metrovick Co-Bo locomotives, but steam traction often substituted for those appalling machines and, in 1965, BR finally faced reality and rostered steam on a regular basis once more! This named train was the last on BR to be regularly steam-hauled.

I hope this album rekindles memories of some of the wonderful atmosphere of the glorious steam era in Lancashire. There was always a real sense of anticipation and excitement evident before a train journey that is not apparent now – happy days indeed! I would like to thank all of the talented photographers who have made available their irreplaceable transparencies for a much wider audience to enjoy. In addition, Chris Evans, David Fakes, Peter Fitton and Tom Heavyside have perused the manuscript and suggested many improvements. I accept full responsibility for any errors that remain.

M. S. W., Burgess Hill, West Sussex, June 2004

The West Coast Main Line

A gleaming Stanier 'Princess Coronation' Class 8P Pacific, No.46245 *City of London*, passes Warrington Bank Quay station with the up 'Royal Scot' on 4th September 1960. The photographer comments that this picture was taken on a Sunday when the train made additional stops and ran considerably later than on weekdays. In the winter 1959/60 timetable the 'Royal Scot' was advertised to leave Glasgow Central at 10.0am on Sundays and arrive in London at 8.15pm, but doubtless the schedule was lengthened for engineering works, the journey being much quicker on weekdays. Warrington is closely situated to the route of the Liverpool & Manchester Railway – which hardly needs an introduction to railway aficionados – and the first line to serve the town was a branch from this route, which opened as early as July 1831. It is recorded that the 'Three Pigeons' inn served as a booking office and waiting room. The origins of Bank Quay station on its present site can be traced back to November 1868, when it replaced an earlier station in another part of the town.   *Alan Chandler*

The Midland Railway Class 3F 0-6-0s are not particularly associated with the north-west of England, but a small number was allocated to Warrington (Dallam) shed. In this June 1960 picture, No.43257 is depicted shunting the sidings at Winwick Quay, on the northern outskirts of Warrington. This was a Johnson design dating back to 1885, and this particular locomotive first saw the light of day when it was outshopped by Neilson & Co. of Glasgow in 1890: it was reboilered twice during its life. During its long career it was shedded at Saltley, Birmingham, in the early 1950s, but was moved to Skipton in May 1952. It saw later service at Lancaster (Green Ayre) shed before transfer to Warrington in November 1959. 43257 was withdrawn in September 1962 and subsequently broken up by Cashmores of Great Bridge, in the West Midlands, in October 1963. *Brian Magilton*

A short section of the WCML in the Warrington area also carries traffic between Manchester and North Wales and is particularly busy, and in steam days a considerable variety of locomotive classes could be observed. Judging by the number of transparencies submitted for this album, it was a magnet for photographers but few are likely to have been fortunate enough to have photographed the machine depicted here. It is 'Black Five' No.44686, one of the very distinctive variants, and this locomotive was one of two (its twin was No.44687) built at Horwich Works during the early days of the BR regime. They were the last LMSR Class 5MTs to be constructed, No.44686 emerging in April 1951 while its sister engine was outshopped during the following month. The locomotives were immediately recognised by their high running plate, massive outside steam pipes, double chimney and Caprotti valve gear. In addition, SKF roller bearing axle boxes were fitted throughout and no doubt due to these refinements these engines reportedly cost an additional £5,000 each to construct. Perhaps due to their being non-standard both locomotives were comparatively early withdrawal victims, No.44686 lasted until October 1965, whilst 44687 was condemned in January 1966. Many of the 'Black Fives' built in the 1930s survived for longer! In this shot No.44686 is seen at Winwick Junction powering (what appears to be) the 7.45am SO Pwllheli to Manchester Exchange on 24th August 1963. The 'Black Five' would probably have replaced a pair of 2-6-4Ts at Llandudno Junction.   *Hugh Ballantyne*

Very few pictures of unrebuilt 'Patriot' Class 6P5F 4-6-0 locomotives were submitted for this book, but here is a portrait of No.45537 *Private E. Sykes V.C.* simmering at Springs Branch shed, Wigan, in October 1959. At the time of this photograph No.45537 was allocated to Carlisle (Upperby) shed where, judging by its disgraceful external condition, it was clearly not the shedmaster's favourite engine. The Class 4F locomotive standing behind it seems to be much more presentable. Constructed at Crewe Works in July 1933, No.45537 lasted in service until June 1962. The last unrebuilt survivors of this distinctive class were condemned later the same year. Many withdrawn steam locomotives, including a 'Princess Coronation', were cut-up at a nearby privately-owned scrap yard and could often be seen on the shed awaiting movement to their last resting place.

P.J. Hughes/Colour-Rail

The steam being emitted by BR Standard 'Britannia' Pacific No.70024 *Vulcan* forms a magnificent column as it leaves Wigan North Western with the 1.46pm train from Barrow-in-Furness to London Euston on a sunny afternoon in February 1967. This working was still diagrammed for steam traction north of Crewe at this time, but diesels reportedly took over from 6th March. The tracks of the Lancashire & Yorkshire Railway's line from Manchester Victoria to Southport and Liverpool Exchange, which serve Wigan Wallgate station, are partially visible to the right of the locomotive. The first line to serve Wigan was the Wigan Branch Railway, which was promoted locally to carry coal and incorporated on 29th May 1830. This seven miles-long line made a junction with the Liverpool & Manchester Railway at Parkside and later became part of the WCML.

Brian Magilton

Wigan has been the butt of jokes for many years, and if ever a Lancashire town had an 'image' problem it is Wigan! Most outsiders probably imagined a depressing, drab and dirty place surrounded by slag heaps and collieries and devoid of any interest. Certainly, the first impression gained by visitors arriving at Wigan's North Western station would have confirmed their worst fears, because during the period covered by this album it was one of the most dilapidated in Lancashire: note the state of the canopies. In fact, unfashionable Wigan has a proud history that can be traced back to 1246. The history of 'Britannia' Pacific No.70052, *Firth of Tay*, seen here powering a Windermere to London train in 1965, does not go back quite as far as that and, in fact, this machine was built at Crewe in 1954. Sadly, it had a very short working life, being withdrawn in March 1967. *Brian Magilton*

A southbound freight train headed by converted Crosti-boilered BR Standard 2-10-0 No.92025 makes a fine sight as it heads past Farington Junction, south of Preston, on 24th July 1965. The locomotive is in quite clean condition, which was unusual for a Class 9F, or indeed any steam locomotive by this date. The line to the right of the signal box is the route to Blackburn, which is still used for freight purposes and by some diverted WCML passenger trains when the route over Shap is closed for any reason. Ten Class 9Fs were equipped with Franco-Crosti boilers when built at Crewe Works in 1955. The idea was that the engines' thermal efficiency would be improved by diverting exhaust gases from the smokebox to heat boiler feed water in a pre-heater drum. The results were disappointing, however, and the locomotives were later converted to run conventionally.

Bill Ashcroft

Stanier Class 5MT No.44897 hurries past Farington Junction with a Heysham to Warrington freight train on 13th May 1968. This machine was built at Crewe Works in September 1945 and lasted until the demise of steam traction in August 1968. The tall structure on the extreme right of the shot is Lostock Hall shed's huge coaling plant, which was a landmark for miles around.

Jeff Mimnagh

Another view of Farington Junction, this time taken looking southwards with the course of the line towards Blackburn clearly visible on the left. The train is a London to Workington express hauled by 'Royal Scot' Class 7P 4-6-0 No.46160 *Queen Victoria's Rifleman*, in sparkling external condition, and this picture was taken on 20th July 1962. At the time this photograph was taken the class was still untouched by withdrawals, but during the ensuing six months nearly half were taken out of service as English Electric Type 4 diesels flooded the WCML, and the survivors could often be seen on quite mundane duties.

Bill Ashcroft

A most interesting picture of a rake of Glasgow suburban electric units, universally known as the 'Blue Trains', being hauled to Horwich Works for repair by Class 9F 2-10-0 No.92093. This photograph was taken at Skew Bridge, south of Preston, on 20th July 1966. The units would have been air-braked and, therefore, not compatible with the vacuum-braked steam locomotive so the train required a brake van on the rear.

Bill Ashcroft

The down 'Lakes Express', with immaculate Stanier 'Princess Coronation' Pacific No.46240 *City of Coventry* in charge, passes an admiring audience of train-spotters at Farington Curve Junction on 29th June 1963. The line to Liverpool, which also gave access to the East Lancashire route, can be seen on the right of the shot. These magnificent locomotives were the pride of the LMSR and hauled the heaviest expresses on the West Coast route until the coming of the diesels. Note the composition of the train which appears to consist entirely of LMSR-designed rolling stock. No.46240 entered traffic following its release from Crewe Works in March 1940 and lasted in service until the sad end of this superb class in September 1964.

Bill Ashcroft

The Hughes/Fowler Class 6P5F 2-6-0s were almost universally popular with locomotive crews, being prodigious steamers, sure-footed and immensely strong when climbing steep gradients. The first example entered traffic in 1926 and the class eventually totalled 245 engines. No.42925, seen here at the south end of Preston station with a long freight train in tow, was one of the later batches to be constructed, being released to service in May 1931. This photograph was taken in September 1964, just two months prior to the engine's withdrawal. Note the army of spotters on the footbridge. *Brian Magilton*

The unmistakable road frontage at the north end of Preston station immediately identifies the location of this photograph which shows the 11.0am London Euston to Carlisle/Workington train pausing with Stanier 'Jubilee' Class 6P5F 4-6-0 No.45578 *United Provinces* in charge. This shot was taken on 8th September 1963, which was a Sunday, probably accounting for the long journey time from London, as the WCML was in the throes of electrification works and consequently schedules were considerably inflated. *Michael Allen*

No album about BR steam in Lancashire would be complete without a shot of a WD 'Austerity' Class 2-8-0, and here No.90720 is seen hurrying along the WCML at Oubeck, south of Lancaster, with a southbound freight in October 1962. These engines were the unglamorous workhorses of heavy freight haulage and rarely in the limelight, so it is remarkable that No.90720 is in such clean condition – perhaps just ex-shops. It probably did not remain in such sparkling condition for long! This locomotive was constructed by Vulcan Foundry (works No.5226) in 1945 and saw service in France as War Department No.79283 before returning to Great Britain in September 1947. One of seventeen taken out of store and placed on loan to BR operating stock in 1948, the locomotive was initially recorded as allocated to Old Oak Common shed in London, but by August 1950, was shedded at Lees (Oldham). By the time of this picture, however, it was based at Lostock Hall shed, just south of Preston. The section of line between Preston and Lancaster was planned by Lancaster merchants who sought to increase the trade of their town and port. They promoted the Lancaster & Preston Junction Railway which opened with the usual celebrations on 25th June 1840.

A.E.R. Cope/Colour-Rail

The LMR maroon-coloured 'sausage' sign immediately identifies the location of this photograph. The train is a Glasgow Central to Manchester Victoria express with Stanier 'Royal Scot' Class 7P 4-6-0 No.46108 *Seaforth Highlander* in charge, and this picture was probably taken in 1962. Water troughs were laid on the level stretch of track just north of Hest Bank station, and on this occasion the tender has overflowed, showering the first coach in the process. The occupants must have been quite surprised by the sudden shower! Comparatively few colour slides were taken of members of this class, perhaps due to the fact that so many examples were condemned in late 1962. By January 1963 nearly half of the original 70 locomotives had gone for scrap, including No.46108 which was withdrawn during that month. Hest Bank station, and nearby Bolton-le-Sands, were closed from 3rd February 1969.

Donald Cash

Photographed in beautiful evening lighting conditions against an uncluttered backdrop of farmland, a London Euston to Carlisle train heads northwards at Hest Bank behind 'Princess Coronation' Class 8P No.46252 *City of Leicester* some time during 1962. No.46252 was built at Crewe in June 1944 and remained in service until May 1963. The single line on the right is the route to Morecambe. The stretch of line northwards from Lancaster was opened as far as Kendal by the Lancaster & Carlisle Railway on 22nd September 1846. Trains from Oxenholme to Carlisle started running on 15th December 1846.

Donald Cash

Carnforth is probably best known as a location of the classic film 'Brief Encounter' parts of which were filmed on the station, where the huge clock, which had a 'starring' role, remains a particular source of interest. To most railway enthusiasts, however, Carnforth will be affectionately remembered as one of steam's last outposts and also for its junction status, with routes fanning out to Barrow-in-Furness in the west and Leeds in the east, in addition to points on the WCML. Sadly, trains on the WCML no longer serve Carnforth following the withdrawal of local services between there and Carlisle and northbound passengers have to begin their journey by travelling southwards to Lancaster. The substantial layout at Carnforth is visible in this picture of 'Black Five' No.44877 accelerating away from the station in bright afternoon sunshine with a Windermere to Blackpool train in August 1964. The mountains of the Lake District can just be discerned on the distant horizon.

David Mitchell

The Longridge Branch

A smartly turned-out former London & North Western Railway 'Super D' 0-8-0, No.49451, stands at Longridge on 22nd September 1962 with the 'Mid-Lancs' rail tour, which was organised by the Railway Correspondence & Travel Society (RCTS). No.49451 was built at Crewe in 1922 as LNWR No.231, but was soon renumbered LMSR No.9451: during its lifetime it was allocated to Nuneaton, Speke Junction (Liverpool) and Springs Branch sheds. Advance publicity in the press ensured that many local people turned out to see the train, but doubtless the organisers had not bargained for four small boys who had to be removed from the locomotive's tender! Later in the day the tour visited

Skipton and the Barnoldswick branch, but with different motive power. The branch line from Preston to Longridge was built with the purpose of conveying stone from Longridge Fell to Preston, this material being required for public buildings in Preston and new docks at Liverpool. Proposals were first made as long ago as 1835 and the 5¾ miles long Preston & Longridge Railway received its Act on 14th July 1836. There was also an inclined plane to quarries at Tootal Height. The opening took place on 1st May 1840, the trains being drawn by horses along the level section. A passenger service was provided, but was an early casualty, being withdrawn from 2nd June 1930.   *Peter Fitton*

Preston to Blackpool North

An account of Lancashire published in 1824 refers to the 'excellent crops of wheat' produced in the Fylde area but says the district is badly in need of communications. In the early 1830s a local Member of Parliament, Mr Peter Hesketh Fleetwood (later Sir Peter), recognised the scope offered by the natural sheltered harbour at the mouth of the river Wyre and it was largely through his efforts that the Preston & Wyre Railway Company (PWR) was incorporated in 1835. The MP laid the first stone of a new industrial town at Burn Naze and engaged an eminent architect to construct a fashionable seaside resort adjacent to the port, which was to be called Fleetwood. The formal opening of the single-track railway took place on 15th July 1840 and fare-paying passengers were conveyed from the following day. The initial service consisted of three trains each way, operated by the North Union Railway. The route was doubled as far as Burn Naze in 1846-47, with the rest being similarly treated in 1875, but it should be noted that part of the line was realigned due to problems with the embankment on the original route. The line to the Fylde leaves the WCML just north of Preston station and in this portrait Stanier Class 5MT No.45353 is seen getting into its stride with the Blackpool portion of the 9.5am London Euston to Carlisle/Blackpool on 26th April 1968. *Bill Ashcroft*

A Blackburn to Blackpool train, hauled by Class 5MT No.45347, heads westwards near Lea Road, just outside Preston, on 30th May 1966. A small wayside station was provided here when the PWR opened, but it was an early closure victim, services being withdrawn from 2nd May 1938.

Jim Davenport/Peter Hutchinson collection

Water troughs were laid between Lea Road and Salwick stations and in this illustration Stanier 'Jubilee' Class 6P5F 4-6-0 No.45565 *Victoria* is depicted passing over the troughs with the 1.25pm Blackpool North to Leeds City train on 9th July 1966. By this date the number of operational 'Jubilees' was down to less than a dozen and few regular passenger turns remained for this once numerous class. Most of the survivors were shedded at depots in the West Riding and No.45565 was one of those locomotives, in this case it was based at Low Moor shed, Bradford, and lasted in traffic until January 1967. During the last year or so of its existence it is likely that *Victoria*'s principal assignments involved nothing more strenuous than local duties, and powering summer Saturday excursion trains of the type seen here. It is, however, fairly certain that the appearance of No.45565 pleased the photographer, especially bearing in mind how thin on the ground these locomotives had become by this time.

Hugh Ballantyne

An intruder on the Fylde! Here, Class K3 2-6-0 No.61853, powering a Lightcliffe, near Bradford, to Blackpool excursion runs almost neck and neck with Class 5MT 4-6-0 No.44731 near Salwick on 23rd April 1962. No.61853 was built at Darlington in 1925 and remained in service until December 1962, when the last of the class was withdrawn from revenue-earning traffic. Despite the fact that the K3s became extinct on the main line at the end of 1962 (one or two survived in departmental service for a time as stationary boilers), the LNER continued to be represented at Blackpool, generally by Class B1 4-6-0s working special trains from the West Riding.

Peter Fitton

Left, above: In this view looking eastwards towards Kirkham and Wesham station, a Stanier Class 5MT, No.44909, is seen heading towards Blackpool North with an unidentified relief train on 15th July 1967. The station is located beyond a road overbridge which is just visible in the background. Note the array of bracket signals controlling the tracks at this point. The carriage immediately behind the locomotive is a LNER Thompson-designed corridor composite (CK) vehicle probably dating from the late-1940s: these coaches were extremely distinctive due to their white, oval-shaped toilet windows. The route from Kirkham to Blackpool South was rather circuitous and on 30th May 1903 a new, direct line was opened to passengers. Known as the 'New Line' or 'Marton Line', summer holiday traffic was so heavy that three intermediate signal boxes were required during this period but, in total contrast, it was very little used in the winter-time. This line diverged from the existing route at Kirkham North Junction: it rejoined the old route at Blackpool South station. The 'new line' was officially closed during November 1965.

Roy Patterson

Left, below: When the railway line from Preston to Fleetwood opened in 1840 a surprisingly large number of passengers chose to alight at Poulton and take a carriage to the embryonic resort of Blackpool. It is recorded that in 1841 a thousand Blackpool passengers made use of this facility on a single Saturday. The branch from Poulton to Blackpool was opened on 29th April 1846 and the coming of the railway transformed this part of the coast. Blackpool's population topped 4,000 in 1861 and the resort's development in the ensuing decades was phenomenal. The promenade was greatly extended and improved, the first tram ran in 1885 while the world-famous tower entertained its first visitors in 1894. By the end of the First World War the LYR was carrying the heaviest holiday traffic in the country, the 'Illuminations' ensuring that the season lasted well into the autumn. In this view Stanier Class 4MT 2-6-4T No.42657 poses at Blackpool North station with a van train on 26th September 1964. At one time this terminus had 15 platforms, some of which were used solely for excursion traffic, but was considerably reduced in size following the construction of a new, brighter, but somewhat characterless, terminus in the mid-1970s. *Michael Allen*

Poulton-le-Fylde to Fleetwood

The 12.0 noon Burnley to Wyre Dock coal train, hauled by Stanier Class 8F 2-8-0 No.48340, heads towards Fleetwood at Poulton on 10th July 1968. An accident at Poulton in 1893 prompted the opening of a new deviation on 28th March 1896, the course of the old PWR line being abandoned. The curve on the right, which enabled trains to travel direct from Blackpool to Fleetwood, came into use on 1st July 1899. A halt, not surprisingly known as Poulton Curve Halt, was constructed on this curve and opened on 1st February 1909. It was closed from 1st December 1952.

Peter Fitton

A very rare colour picture of the original terminus at Fleetwood, showing Stanier Class 4MT 2-6-4T No.42461 awaiting departure with the 2.35pm train to Preston on 3rd September 1963. By the mid-1840s Fleetwood had developed as a packet station with sailings to the Isle of Man, Belfast, Dublin and Ardrossan. The last-mentioned was a popular route from London to Scotland until the opening of the WCML in 1848. In order to cater for the increasing ferry traffic, the existing Fleetwood station was closed in July 1883 and an extension opened to new premises adjacent to the quay, thus enabling easy transfer for rail passengers. Prior to the First World War the Belfast service, in particular, was extremely popular and boat trains operated from London, and Leeds via Manchester. The latter conveyed corridor stock and included a dining car. Belfast steamer sailings continued until improvements were made to the Heysham service in 1928, whilst the Isle of Man ferries lasted until 1961, when expensive repairs to the quay were required. Fleetwood also became the busiest fishing port on the west coast. The station seen here was closed on 18th April 1966 and Wyre Dock station, which was convenient for the town centre, renamed Fleetwood. These arrangements lasted only until 1st June 1970, when the passenger trains between Poulton and Fleetwood were withdrawn.

Michael Allen

Kirkham to Blackpool Central

Lytham was established as a sea bathing resort in the early years of the nineteenth century, the population in 1821 being 1,300. Lytham Pool, a mile to the east, was a transhipment point for cargoes bound for Preston. In 1841 a small dock was opened and the PWR decided that it might be worthwhile to lay a branch from Kirkham, which was opened on 16th February 1846. The Lytham to Blackpool line was the responsibility of a separate company, the Blackpool & Lytham Railway, which was incorporated on 17th May 1861. The line carried its first fare-paying customers on 6th April 1863, but was not physically connected to the line from Kirkham until July 1874, by which time the PWR had been absorbed by the LYR and LNWR. In more recent times this route has been dramatically downgraded in status. Blackpool Central was closed in 1964, and in 1970 the through London services were diverted to Blackpool North. Subsequently the line has been singled and now has a purely local service. Lying snow gives an extra dimension to this picture of Class 5MT No.45212 leaving Lytham with the Blackpool portion of the 9.5am ex-Euston on 9th February 1968.

Peter Fitton

Photographed shortly after departure from Ansdell and Fairhaven station, the 4.40pm Liverpool Exchange to Blackpool Central train is seen hurrying along behind BR Standard Class 4MT 4-6-0 No.75032 on 10th August 1964. From Lytham to Blackpool the railway traverses an almost continuous built-up residential area, a totally different landscape from 'industrial' Lancashire. *Peter Fitton*

Stanier Class 5MT No.45227, in presentably clean condition, pulls away from St. Annes station with the Blackpool portion of the 9.35am from London Euston on 16th August 1967. This section of line is noteworthy for the various wayside stations and halts which were opened to tap potential sources of local traffic. A station called Stony Hill (near the present Squires Gate) was brought into use on 1st April 1865, but was closed seven years later. On 1st October 1913 halts were opened at Burlington Road and Gillett's Crossing following the introduction of a railmotor service between Blackpool Central and Lytham. Both were closed for the duration of the First World War, but reopened on 1st March 1920. They were finally closed permanently on 1st January 1949.

Peter Fitton

Blackpool Tower immediately identifies the location of this illustration, which shows a busy scene with two trains awaiting departure on 27th September 1964. The locomotives are BR Standard Class 7P6F 'Britannia' Pacific No.70005 *John Milton* and Stanier Class 5MT No.44826. In the early days of the Blackpool to Kirkham line the station here was known as Hound's Hill, but its name was altered to Blackpool Central in June 1878. In 1861, as previously mentioned, Blackpool's population was a mere 4,000, but its remarkable growth as a holiday destination sparked massive development and by the end of the century the population was nearing 50,000. It was also a very agreeable place to live and became extremely fashionable with Lancashire's middle classes. In 1895 the first 'Club' carriages were run between Blackpool Central and Manchester Victoria for businessmen, these 'Residential' trains being composed of the latest corridor stock which was luxuriously appointed. Use of the exclusive 'Club' coaches was confined to a limited number of first class ticket holders, who paid an extra supplement. Blackpool Central station was closed a few weeks after this picture was taken.

Michael Allen

Preston to Colne

A train from Blackpool to Lincoln, probably the 10.45am SO ex-Blackpool Central, leaves Preston behind Stanier Class 5MT No.45436 in September 1964. The other locomotive visible is one of the same designer's Class 4MT 2-6-4Ts, No.42662, which is heading a local train. This shot provides a bird's-eye view of the eastern side of Preston station, which has since been completely swept away; trains to and from Blackburn now travel via Lostock Hall, Farington Curve Junction and the WCML. Even in BR days the platforms seen here were still referred to by local operating staff as the East Lancashire side of the station, while the 'main' part of the station, largely served by trains on the WCML, was known as the North Union side. This was despite the fact that these companies ceased to exist in 1859 and 1888 respectively!

Brian Magilton

The skyline of Preston stands out on the horizon as Stanier Class 8F 2-8-0 No.48423 takes the 6.40pm Preston to Healey Mills freight. The sight and sound of Class 8F locomotives working freight trains in this area had been an everyday occurrence for many years, but this portrait was taken on 2nd August 1968, the last weekday of BR steam, so this picture, taken near Farington, is of special interest. This train was reportedly the final steam-hauled freight working over this stretch of line, the last ever such train on BR being a working from Heysham to Carnforth the following day. The Preston & Blackburn Railway Company was incorporated on 6th June 1844, the line opening for business on 1st June 1846.   *Roy Hobbs*

Right, above: Count the chimney pots in this panoramic illustration of the 'townscape' of Accrington! Class 5MT No.45407, its train still snaking across the viaduct, eases into Accrington station with an evening Colne to Preston parcels train in late July 1968. The train is entering a former Bury line platform which was used as a small parcels depot. It would have reversed out and continued to Preston by way of the tracks on the left. The first railway to reach the town was the line from Blackburn which opened on 19th June 1848, one of the intermediate stations being the delightfully named Church & Oswaldtwistle. Two months later the link from Stubbins, on the steeply graded route from Bury, also opened to passenger traffic. This climbed to a summit of 771ft. above sea level at Baxenden and boasted fearsome gradients of 1 in 38. *David Mitchell*

Right, below: Photographed in brilliant evening sunshine, Class 8F No.48448, complete with a snowplough, dashes through Huncoat station with a short freight working in June 1968. Note the maroon station signs and gas lighting, plus the whitewashed flower tubs and stonework on the platforms. The backdrop of terraced houses, not to mention the tall power station chimneys and cooling towers, are typical of this area of industrial Lancashire. *David Mitchell*

Following the end of steam traction across the northern fells to Carlisle at the end of 1967, steam was confined to its last refuge in north-west England and routes which had previously been largely ignored by enthusiasts suddenly took on a greater significance. The line from Preston to the East Lancashire towns of Blackburn, Burnley and Colne was one of these, and even though its best friends would never describe it as the prettiest route in England, it gained a higher profile as steam retreated from other, more spectacular, routes. There was a considerable amount of steam activity on freight workings, principally coal trains to Wyre Dock and the return 'empties' of course. In addition, one or two van trains also operated to give extra variety. In this picture, Class 8F No.48348, in very clean condition, is hardly likely to be exerted by its modest load as it leaves Rose Grove with a westbound freight in tow during the last days of steam. The junction with the branch to Padiham is just discernible in the background.

David Mitchell

The spotless red buffer beam, white-painted buffers plus smokebox door fittings, and, needless to say, the generally immaculate condition of the locomotive, immediately identify this picture as one taken during the last few days of steam activity. The train is a Colne to Preston parcels, which is pictured approaching Burnley Barracks station on 1st August 1968. The last hours of steam were hectic for many enthusiasts as they hurried from place to place trying to record the final, history-making movements of each locomotive. Surely, the shot seen here of No.45110 in glorious evening sunshine made it all worthwhile? Steam traction made its debut at Burnley in September 1848, when the line from Accrington opened, and bowed out after nearly 120 years faithful service, three days after this shot was taken.   *David Mitchell*

Blackburn to Hellifield

Stanier Class 4MT 2-6-4T No.42484 enters Wilpshire station with the 5.10pm train from Hellifield to Blackburn on 28th July 1962. The line from Blackburn to Hellifield was proposed by the Blackburn, Clitheroe & North Western Junction Railway which received the Royal Assent in July 1846. It was intended to connect with the proposed North Western Railway near Hellifield, as its title suggests. The first sod was cut by Lord Ribblesdale at Clitheroe on 30th December 1846, but after that construction proceeded slowly. After much delay, the first section of the route was eventually opened as far as Chatburn on 21st June 1850 for single line working only. The line is well-known for several heavy engineering works, notably a 325 yards-long tunnel at Wilpshire, and Whalley viaduct, which consists of 48 spans. It was not until the Midland Railway (MR) started construction of the Settle to Carlisle route that further efforts were made to extend the line from Chatburn to Hellifield, and this part of the route, which is mostly in Yorkshire and outside the scope of this book, opened throughout in 1880.   *Roy Patterson*

Some local lads chat to the crew of Fairburn-designed Class 4MT 2-6-4T No.42147 as its awaits departure from Chatburn with the 4.10pm Hellifield to Blackburn train. This picture was also taken on 28th July 1962. Trains terminated at Gisburn from June 1879 to June 1880 when through running into the MR's new Hellifield station commenced. The opening of the Blackburn to Hellifield line throughout provided a new route from Lancashire to Scotland which the enterprising MR was quick to exploit, and during the period up to the start of the First World War this line saw a steady stream of express trains which linked Liverpool and Manchester with Scotland via the Settle & Carlisle line. Following the grouping in 1923 the route declined in status, but a summer Saturday Manchester to Glasgow train continued to be routed this way until the mid-1960s. Local passenger services ceased in September 1962, but the line is still open throughout for freight traffic and occasional diverted passenger workings. The section from Blackburn to Clitheroe has had its local passenger trains restored.   *Roy Patterson*

Burnley to Todmorden

Careful use of a telephoto lens has produced this striking shot of Stanier Class 8F 2-8-0 No.48062 climbing to Copy Pit summit, between Burnley and Todmorden, with an eastbound train of empty coal wagons in April 1968. This highly scenic line climbed to an altitude of 749 feet above sea level, and spectacular pictures could be obtained of steam locomotives heaving freight trains up to the summit. Bankers were usually employed over the gruelling 1 in 65 west-bound section from Stansfield Hall, near Todmorden. Like the East Lancashire line, this was another route that only came to the attention of photographers towards the end of steam, perhaps because of its rather irregular passenger service. In its heyday there were six intermediate stations, but the population served was very thin and the first station to be closed, Holme, was shut as long ago as 1930, with the rest of the stations following at various times during the ensuing thirty years. Despite the loss of its local passenger services, the route continued to be busy with seasonal trains from the West Riding to Blackpool and heavy coal workings from Yorkshire collieries, as already mentioned. The collapse of the coal industry in the 1980s has dramatically reduced the line's importance for freight, but passenger traffic is buoyant following the introduction of an all-year-round Leeds to Blackpool service. *Derek Huntriss*

Southport to Preston

Right, above: The distinctive overall roof and electric unit lurking in the background provide instant clues to the identity of this location – Southport Chapel Street station. This picture shows Fairburn-designed Class 4MT 2-6-4T No.42061 awaiting departure with the 9.17am train to Preston on 8th September 1963. The line from Southport to Preston was promoted by the West Lancashire Railway which was incorporated on 14th August 1871. Its objective was to build a route linking the two towns that followed the south shore of the River Ribble estuary. The line was opened in a piecemeal manner, the first, isolated stretch from Hesketh Bank to Hesketh Park coming into operation on 19th February 1878. On 10th June of the same year an extension to a temporary terminus at Southport Windsor Road (later Ash Street) was brought into use, whilst on 18th May 1882 the northern end of the line was extended across the River Douglas to Longton. The entire line was operational later the same year, the short section from Southport Ash Street to Central on 4th September whilst the gap at the northern end was bridged on 16th September when the Longton to Preston stretch was opened to passengers. *Michael Allen*

Right, below: Churchtown station, located 2¹/2 miles from Southport Chapel Street station, was unlikely to have been busy due to competition from local buses, and in any case the trains were handicapped by the somewhat circuitous route taken by the railway between there and Southport. Here, Stanier 'Jubilee' Class 6P5F 4-6-0 No.45600 *Bermuda* coasts into the station with a Preston-bound train on 7th September 1963. In the winter 1959 timetable thirteen trains a day were advertised between Southport and Preston on weekdays. *Michael Allen*

Left, above: Crossens station on 7th September 1963, showing the 10.0am Southport to Preston train entering the station with Stanier Class 4MT 2-6-4T No.42435 in charge. This machine was built in March 1936 at Derby Works and gave exactly 29 years service before being withdrawn in March 1965. In Victorian times Southport became a popular residential town for businessmen working in Liverpool and Manchester, and was also attracting increasing numbers of holiday visitors. These developments prompted the electrification of the line from Liverpool by the LYR, plus the short section on to Crossens to serve the town's northern suburbs, the latter opening in 1904. This accounts for the third rail visible in this shot which, at first sight, looks as though it was taken somewhere on the Southern Region!
Michael Allen

Left, below: A scene at New Longton and Hutton station, recorded on 26th August 1964, showing a Preston to Southport local train running in behind Fowler Class 4MT 2-6-4T No.42369. The station was opened in 1889 as Howick, but was renamed Hutton & Howick in 1898. In November 1924 the railway authorities decided that a further change of name was necessary and the station's name was altered to New Longton and Hutton. The northern part of the route traversed a remote and sparsely-populated, but very fertile, part of Lancashire famous for its market gardening activities. This rural line probably never paid its way at any time during its life, so there was no surprise when it was tabled for closure in the Beeching Report. Closure came from 7th September 1964 and it is recorded that the final passenger working was the 10.20pm from Southport to Preston on 6th September, which consisted of seven well-filled carriages hauled by 2-6-4T No.42296. Electric services also ceased at the same time, one of the few closures of an electrified line that has ever taken place in Great Britain.
Bill Ashcroft

A fascinating interior view of Preston station taken on 5th September 1963. Stanier-designed Class 4MT 2-6-4T No.42435 stands at Platform No.8 with the empty coaches of the 10.0am train from Southport. A sister engine, which had presumably powered the train from Southport, can just be discerned in the distance. Note the array of station signs in LMR colours. Railway development at Preston can be traced back to the early 1830s, when local manufacturers promoted the Preston & Wigan Railway which received the Royal Assent on 22nd April 1831. It was the intention to link up with the Wigan Branch Railway, but insufficient financial support was forthcoming and the two companies subsequently combined in May 1834 to form the North Union Railway. This was the first railway amalgamation in Great Britain. The directors travelled over the whole line to Parkside (on the Liverpool & Manchester Railway) on 21st October 1838 and the line opened to the public ten days later. This development immediately gave the town railway communication with London, then 218 miles away via Birmingham.

Michael Allen

Aintree to Southport

If any rail-served location in Lancashire was definitely off the beaten track it was Altcar, a little-known station on the line from Aintree to Southport. In this picture Class 7F 0-8-0 No.49434 poses there, on weed-infested track, with a rail tour on 6th June 1959. This train started from Liverpool Riverside station, which handled boat train traffic, and visited Ormskirk, Rainford, St. Helens and Widnes before terminating at Liverpool Lime Street. Powers to construct the line through Altcar were obtained in August 1881 and it opened in September 1884. On 1st November 1887 Altcar became a junction when a line from Meols

Cop was opened by the grandly named Liverpool, Southport & Preston Junction Railway. The thinly populated agricultural countryside in this area proved to be infertile territory for these lines, however, and Altcar's status as a junction proved short-lived, the section to Downholland, on the Meols Cop line, closing in November 1926. The rest of this line followed in September 1938. The Aintree to Southport route lost its passenger service from 7th January 1952, but sections remained open for freight. It is recorded that the track on this line had been completely lifted by the end of 1960: perhaps this was the last train. *Roy Patterson*

Liverpool Exchange to Preston

A scene at Liverpool Exchange station, showing Stanier Class 5MT No.44950 waiting to leave for Kirkdale sidings with the empty stock of an arrival from Glasgow. This picture was taken on 19th May 1968. The Liverpool, Ormskirk & Preston Railway obtained its Act on 18th August 1846, possibly as a result of strong backing by the East Lancashire Railway (ELR), with which it amalgamated two months later. The Liverpool & Bury Railway had already been incorporated, on 31st July 1845, and this company was soon absorbed by the Manchester & Leeds Railway, which became the LYR in 1847. The ELR and LYR were fierce rivals and so these two companies, both converging on Liverpool, were in opposing camps. Despite the hostility between them, they were able to agree that their respective routes should meet at Walton, and that the line thence into Liverpool should be jointly owned. The LYR line was brought into use on 20th November 1848, whilst the ELR opened on 2nd April 1849. Initially, they failed to agree on a name for their new joint terminus, to the ELR it was known as Great Howard Street, while the LYR called it Borough Gaol. Powers had been granted for a new terminus half a mile nearer the centre of Liverpool, but the ELR was strongly in favour of abandoning them while its rival was very keen to proceed. The LYR's wise policy to press on won the day and the new station, designed by Sir John Hawksmoor in the Italian style, opened on 13th May 1850. Each company had its own booking office, refreshment and waiting rooms and there were even two large iron roofs! The premises were replaced by a new Exchange station on the same site in 1884-88.

Bill Ashcroft

During the last months of steam the hitherto obscure Liverpool to Preston line, which had always been overshadowed by the WCML, gained a higher profile due to the exploits of enginemen on the few remaining steam turns. The 9.0am Liverpool Exchange to Preston and 9.25pm return (to and from Glasgow) were often steam-worked on weekdays, while two services were booked for steam on Sundays. On 19th May 1968 the 4.53pm SuO from Preston, hauled by 'Black Five' No.44950, reached Ormskirk (15¼ miles from Preston) in 17mins. 43secs, with a top speed of 77mph at Rufford. Further high speed running followed with a maximum of 80mph after Maghull, and Orrell

Park, 8¼ miles from Ormskirk was passed in the very creditable time of 8mins. 33secs. Similar impressive performances were recorded whenever steam traction appeared depending, of course, on the mechanical condition of the locomotive and enthusiasm of the crew. The very last ordinary steam passenger train in Great Britain was the 9.25pm from Preston to Liverpool on 3rd August and Preston station was thronged with people when it pulled out with 'Black Five' No.45318 in charge: an historic moment in the annals of steam power. In this shot No.45212 races through Croston on Sunday 14th April with the 9.50am from Liverpool Exchange to Glasgow Central.

Jeff Mimnagh

Locomotives employed on the passenger turns radiating from Preston benefited from unofficial cleaning by enthusiasts, and a fortunate recipient of this lavish attention was apparently Stanier Class 5MT No.44713. Here it creates a really stirring sight near Midge Hall with the 4.53pm SuO Preston to Liverpool Exchange train on a sunny 7th April 1968. There is a slight downhill gradient here in favour of southbound trains, but shortly after Rufford the line starts to climb on gradients as steep as 1 in 129 to a summit at Aughton Park.

Jeff Mimnagh

Lancaster to Morecambe and Heysham

Left, above: A westbound freight train, powered by Class 5MT No.45196, passes through Lancaster Green Ayre station on 6th September 1963. This station was located on the south bank of the River Lune, which is out of sight on the left of the picture. The first trains from this station ran to Poulton-le-Sands (near Morecambe) on 12th June 1848, while the line eastwards towards Wennington opened on 17th November 1849. This route was extended in stages, through running to the 'main' Ingleton to Skipton line at Clapham commencing on 1st June 1850. On 3rd January 1966 passenger services from the West Riding to Morecambe via Lancaster were withdrawn and Lancaster Green Ayre station was consigned to history. A railway journey from Skipton to Morecambe is still possible however, the trains running via Carnforth.   *Michael Allen*

Left, below: A Heysham to Stourton (near Leeds) freight train is depicted between Morecambe and Scale Hall in October 1965. The latter station had a very short career, being opened in June 1957 to serve new housing development, but closed in 1966. Motive power is provided by Stanier 'Jubilee' Class 6P5F 4-6-0 No.45675 *Hardy* which later became noteworthy as one of the last-surviving members of its class, based at Holbeck shed, Leeds. At first sight this location could easily be mistaken as somewhere on one of the double track sections of the WCML but, of course, the odd support masts for the overhead catenary provide contrary evidence. Electrification of this line dates from 1908, when the MR experimentally introduced the single phase a.c. system at 6,600 volts, 25 cycles with overhead collection. It was the pioneer system of its type in Great Britain and one of the first in the world. The equipment had become life-expired by 1950 and, following a visit by a BR delegation to France, it was decided to convert the line to the industrial frequency of 50 cycles. To enable this work to be carried out electric services were replaced by steam from February 1951 to August 1953, when 'new' refurbished units formerly used on the Willesden Junction to Earls Court line took over. One of the curiosities of this line were the wooden support masts, this being the only route in Great Britain on which they were used.
David Mitchell

Right, above: If asked to name the location of this picture most railway enthusiasts would probably be very confused by the (apparently) quadruple track main line and non-standard overhead gantries. It is difficult to believe that this picture was taken just east of Morecambe Promenade station and actually shows three separate routes. The tracks on the far left go to Carnforth via Bare Lane, whilst the two lines immediately behind the locomotive are those of the erstwhile line to Lancaster Green Ayre. The lines on the right lead to Heysham Harbour. The picture was taken in 1965, not long before the electric service was withdrawn, and the train, hauled by Ivatt Class 2MT 2-6-2T No.41251, appears to be a local freight working. Morecambe Euston Road station was located behind the large shed on the left. *David Mitchell*

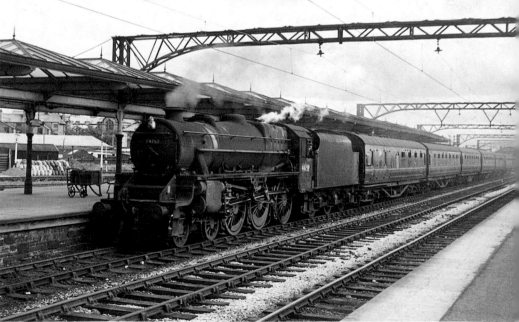

Right, below: No prizes for identifying this location, the station's 'sausage' sign, not to mention the distinctive overhead electrification gantries, immediately give it away! This portrait of Morecambe Promenade station was recorded on 6th September 1963 and shows a rather begrimed Stanier Class 5MT, No.44758, drawing to a halt with the 10.47am train from Leeds. At the time of this picture the line between Lancaster, Morecambe and Heysham still had a special, individual character, perhaps because of the overhead electrics, but does not seem to have been widely photographed. Maybe enthusiasts found the lure of steam over Shap just too irresistible, or possibly they were deterred by the electrification poles! *Michael Allen*

The MR had ambitious plans for Heysham Harbour, a proposal for a port being first mooted in 1896. More than £3 million was spent on the works which eventually covered 350 acres. Local passenger operations started on 11th July 1904 and were electrified four years later. Steamer sailings to Belfast commenced on 1st September 1904 and sailings from Morecambe to Dublin and Londonderry were transferred to Heysham on the same date. The following year a service to Douglas was inaugurated and both this, and the Belfast boat, had express train connections from London St. Pancras. The Belfast service rose in popularity, and in 1935 a fourth new vessel was introduced. Another factor in the growth of railway traffic was the development of Air Ministry, Shell oil and chemical installations at Heysham Moss, which was covered by private sidings. The Belfast boats ran until 1975, but a service still operates to the Isle of Man, complete with train connections, so the line to Heysham continues to see some modest passenger traffic. Here, 'Black Five' No.45287 is seen at Heysham prior to working a freight train to Carnforth on 2nd August 1968, just a few days before the demise of steam.   *Donald Cash*

Lancaster to Wennington

A shot of 'The Ribble-Lune' rail tour, powered by BR Standard Class 6P5F 'Clan' Pacific No.72007 *Clan Mackintosh*, passing Ladies Walk sidings, Lancaster, on 23rd May 1964. This leisurely afternoon jaunt covered many secondary routes, and lightly-used spur lines, in north Lancashire, plus a short venture into Yorkshire. The train started from Preston and ran along the old West Lancashire line (closure of which had just been announced) as far as Roe Lane Junction, where the route to Meols Cop was taken. The train eventually reached the Liverpool to Preston line, by virtue of traversing the north curve to Burscough

North Junction, and later headed for Gisburn, on the Blackburn to Hellifield route, where it halted for photographic purposes. Running via Settle Junction and Lancaster (Green Ayre), the participants' next stop was Heysham Harbour, where they took a breath of sea air before visiting Lancaster (Old) station, the original terminus of the Preston & Lancaster Railway. On the last leg of the trip back to Preston the train reached a maximum speed of 64½ mph, to conclude what must have been a very enjoyable ramble along some routes long since completely closed. *Donald Cash*

Prior to the closure of the route via Lancaster (Green Ayre) in January 1966, some trains from the West Riding to Carnforth/Morecambe divided at Wennington, a rural country junction station if ever there was one. This station is just inside the Lancashire border, the remainder of this secondary route being in Yorkshire. Here, Stanier 2-6-4T No.42464 awaits departure with the three-coach Carnforth portion of a train from Leeds on a damp and dismal 28th June 1963. Note that the steam heating appears to be functioning, so it must have been an unseasonably cold day.

David Mitchell

The Glasson Dock Branch

In 1826 a branch of the Lancaster canal opened to Glasson Dock, which is located on the south bank of the River Lune estuary, about seven miles south-west of Lancaster. This development had the effect of diverting shipping and, therefore, potential railway traffic from Lancaster, but the railway authorities of the day ignored the situation until the London & North Western Railway (LNWR) proposed a branch from Lancaster in the early 1880s. It opened to goods traffic in April 1883 and to passengers from 9th July. There was only one public intermediate station, at Conder Green, but a private platform was provided at Ashton Hall for the use of Lord Ashton, a local landowner. The line served a thinly populated area and passenger trains ceased from 7th July 1930, although freight traffic continued until 1964, after

which a short section remained at Lancaster giving access to the quay. In this illustration, the Railway Correspondence & Travel Society's 'Glasson Dock Brake Van Special', with Ivatt Class 2MT No.46433 in charge, is seen at the terminus on 20th June 1964, with participants wandering about admiring the view, and doubtless mindful of the fact that they would be unlikely to see another train at this spot. The weather-beaten station building is visible. It is recorded that BR staff had to search in the long grass to find the point lever before the train could retrace its steps to Lancaster. Even then, only slow progress was possible initially due to the locomotive continually slipping on the overgrown and rusty track. *Bill Ashcroft*

Carnforth to Barrow

A general view of Carnforth shed yard, or 'motive power depot' to give it its official title, taken on 25th September 1967. The position of the Carnforth station to Barrow-in-Furness line is marked by the bracket signal, whilst the location of the avoiding line, which provides a direct connection from Hellifield to Barrow, is indicated by the tank wagons just visible on the left of the picture. Electrification of parts of the WCML and the introduction of hundreds of diesels, not to mention the effects of line closures, were having a devastating effect on the remaining steam classes and, indeed, most of the locomotives seen here appear to be stored. At the time of this picture, steam traction's sphere of operation at Carnforth was declining, the end of steam in the Leeds area for example, a week after this scene was recorded, no doubt caused a drop in workings towards Hellifield. At the end of December 1967 steam workings over Shap summit to Carlisle ceased, bringing to an end one of the most magnificent spectacles of steam operations in Great Britain. Steam engines remained in use in small numbers, however, on all of the other routes radiating from Carnforth until final withdrawal in August 1968, by which time the shed had become a place of pilgrimage for enthusiasts from throughout the country.

Gerald Daniels

Right, above: In this illustration, taken just a hundred yards or so from the previous view, a typically unkempt Class WD 2-8-0, No.90681, rounds the curve from Carnforth station with a freight bound for Barrow-in-Furness in August 1964. The locomotive shed is out of sight on the right. This machine was assembled by Vulcan Foundry in 1944 (works No.5158) and was shipped to France bearing its War Department number 79215. It returned home in 1947 only to be stored by the Ministry of Supply at Kingham in the Cotswolds. It remained in store long after most of its sister engines had entered BR service, but was in traffic by mid-1949, based on the LMR. No.90681 appears to have spent its entire working life on that region, being based in Lancashire at Fleetwood, Lostock Hall and Rose Grove sheds at various times. *David Mitchell*

Right, below: BR Standard Class 4MT No.75048 is depicted near Silverdale station on 1st August 1968, a few days before the elimination of BR steam traction, heading westwards with a freight train from Carnforth. This locomotive was regularly used for shunting purposes at Ulverston during the final week of steam operation, so perhaps that was its destination. No.75048 doubtless appeared on this working the following day, but was then unceremoniously consigned to the dump at Carnforth shed, its short working career having come to an end. It was one of three members of the class that achieved a degree of fame as a result of their appearances on the scenic Grassington branch, near Skipton, for which they were kept in clean condition by local photographers. *Roy Hobbs*

The 2.45pm Durham to Ulverston train, with Fairburn Class 4MT 2-6-4T No.42673 in charge, pauses at Grange-over-Sands on 8th July 1960. This was a most unusual, and quite fascinating, working which ran only on alternate Fridays solely for the benefit of mine-workers going to convalesce in either Grange-over-Sands or Ulverston. During its journey the train travelled over the magnificent Stainmore route across the Pennines and changed engines at Tebay, on this occasion No.42673 replacing Ivatt Class 2MT 2-6-0 No.46458. From Tebay the train then threaded the Lune gorge, and passed over Grayrigg summit, before branching off the WCML at Hincaster Junction. From there it ran over the little-known route to Arnside, which lost its passenger trains way back in 1953. So, a substantial proportion of the route traversed by this train was not used by advertised passenger workings. The line between Arnside and Kents Bank stations, which runs close to the shore, is rarely out of sight of Morecambe Bay and must have been a cheering sight for the miners looking forward to a fortnight's recuperation by the sea.

John Langford

This portrait, taken at Ulverston on 18th April 1961, shows an unidentified Barrow-in-Furness train pulling out of the station behind Fowler-designed Class 4MT 2-6-4T No.42420, which is in excellent external condition. This particular locomotive was one of the comparatively small number of Fowler engines built with a side window cab. No.42420 was a product of Derby Works from where it emerged in December 1933. It lasted in service until May 1962. The column of steam in the background is being emitted by No.58177, a veteran Class 2F 0-6-0 the history of which goes back to the 1870s.

Barrow shed was one of the last outposts of these locomotives, where a small contingent was maintained for local shunting duties, including trips on the Lake Side branch which diverges from the Carnforth to Barrow route near Ulverston. The last-mentioned town first appeared on a railway map in 1854 when it was reached by a local line from Dalton, but there was no route eastwards at that time towards Carnforth giving access to the WCML. This situation was rectified in 1857 when the Ulverston & Lancaster Railway was opened.

Bill Ashcroft

The Lake Side Branch

A branch from Ulverston to Newby Bridge was promoted by the Furness Railway (FR) which obtained an Act on 16th July 1866. This seven miles-long single track line had a double track triangular junction with the Carnforth to Barrow route 1½ miles east of Ulverston station. Goods trains to Newby Bridge commenced on 23rd April 1869. The FR saw the potential of linking up with the Lake Windermere steamers, but decided that it would be unwise to use the existing berth at Newby Bridge because vessels would have to navigate the unpredictable headwaters of the River Leven. So, the FR vowed to construct a purpose-built quay at Lake Side and this was commissioned on 1st June 1869, from which date passenger services along the entire branch commenced operation. During the period before the start of the First World War tourist and excursion traffic made the branch extremely prosperous, but winter

steamer trips on the lake ceased in the early 1920s and this development presaged the slow decline in the branch's fortunes. All-year-round passenger services ceased from 26th September 1938 and were withdrawn completely during most of the Second World War period. On 3rd June 1946 summer trains resumed, but this kind of seasonal operation made the line extremely vulnerable to the harsh economic realities of the early 1960s and the line was closed from 6th September 1965. In this shot Class 5MT No.44877 simmers at Lake Side after arrival with a local working in August 1964.

Modern-day travellers can still ride on part of the branch as the Lakeside & Haverthwaite Railway runs steam trains for 3½ miles from Haverthwaite through Newby Bridge to its terminus at Lakeside.

David Mitchell

Manchester Victoria to Southport

First-time visitors to mainland Great Britain from Northern Ireland could have been forgiven for thinking that their train had made an unscheduled stop in the middle of a forgotten bomb site, such was the appalling condition of parts of Manchester Victoria station by the late 1960s. If there had been a national competition to find the grubbiest and most derelict looking main line station it would surely have been a strong contender. But, despite its drawbacks, this ramshackle, scruffy old place had an atmosphere all of its own. The totally unintelligible train announcements which seemed to echo all around, the constant smell from the local brewery intermingled with the rather different odour of a Newton Heath 'Black Five', all seemed to combine to give the station a unique character not found elsewhere. Perhaps the most thrilling experience at Victoria station occurred when a heavy trans-Pennine express departed from Exchange station. These traversed Victoria on the through line, and in steam days enginemen took a run at the 1 in 59 Miles Platting bank, with the result that the station's comparative calm was shattered, first of all by the train engine exerting maximum effort and then, after a few seconds, by the banker being flogged mercilessly. Happy days! Here the last 'Belfast Boat Express' is pictured after arrival on 5th May 1968 with partly cleaned-up Class 5MT No.45025 in charge. *Donald Cash*

Stanier Class 5MT No.44766 stands in Platform 14 at Manchester Victoria after arrival with the 9.2am from Newcastle on 17th July 1966. A station has existed on this site since 1844 when the Manchester & Leeds and Liverpool & Manchester railways joined forces to construct a through station near Hunts Bank, and Victoria station was established where the routes met. Nearby Exchange station was built in 1884 as a result of congestion at Victoria, the stations being connected by the 2,194 feet-long Platform 11 which was the longest in the country. Victoria station underwent extensive alterations at various times in LYR days, most particularly in 1904 when the premises took the shape that lasted until the early 1990s. Perhaps the bleakest time in the station's history was the night of 23rd December 1940 when German bombers devastated part of the roof and offices, including a vital traffic control section. The area seen here was especially badly affected, the roof being totally destroyed: it was never replaced. Fifty years afterwards scorched timbers and damaged ironwork were still visible.

Jim Davenport

Right, above: Trains from Manchester to Southport normally travelled on the old LYR route from Manchester to Wigan Wallgate via Atherton, which was opened in stages in the late 1880s. The line was opened throughout on 1st October 1888, while the Wigan avoiding line, from Hindley to Pemberton, was brought into use on 1st June 1889. Wigan Wallgate station, which dates from February 1896, was the third LYR station in the town. The first two were apparently severely criticised by local people as being unworthy of the town and were closed. The LYR route from Wigan to Southport, which dates from 9th April 1855, passes through some attractive, rural countryside, this area of Lancashire being extremely fertile. Here, BR Standard Class 4MT 4-6-0 No.75046 eases away from Wigan Wallgate station with a Liverpool to Rochdale local train in June 1965.

Brian Magilton

Right, below: A Southport to Manchester train, headed by Stanier Class 5MT No.44756, waits to leave Southport Chapel Street station in April 1964. Note that the three carriages (the others appear to be detached) forming this fairly long distance service are of the non-corridor type. No.44756, built at Crewe in 1948, was very different in appearance to the 'standard' engines in the class. It was constructed with Caprotti valve gear, a double chimney and Timken roller bearings. In addition, its boiler was two inches higher than usual, the extra height being emphasised by the fact that the running plate was lower. Perhaps the most unattractive design feature of all were the huge outside steam pipes and the result was an exceedingly ugly looking machine. At the time of this photograph No.44756 was based at Southport shed, but survived only for a further six months in service.

Brian Magilton

Irwell Street Goods Depot (Salford)

Former LYR Class 21 0-4-0ST No.51232 simmers at the somewhat basic coaling stage in Irwell Street goods yard, Salford, some time in April 1963. This yard, and also the adjacent New Bailey goods depot, were situated beneath the partially visible viaduct of the former LNWR route from Manchester Exchange to Warrington. The diminutive locomotive was an Aspinall design dating from 1891, and this example was built in 1906. At the time of this picture only four of these locomotives remained in BR stock, of which two – the other was No.51237 – were based at Agecroft shed, solely to shunt the yard at Irwell Street which had unbelievably tight curves. The engine was booked to be available at Irwell Street from early on a Monday morning

until Saturday lunchtime, when it returned to its home shed with the yard pilot locomotive. This was usually a Class 3F 'Jinty' 0-6-0T, but Fowler short wheelbase 0-6-0T dock tank No.47165 was noted on occasions. The pilot locomotive was also ideally suited to the tightly-curved track, but was prohibited from the worst sections, where only the 'Pug' ventured. Its principal job was to work short trains of wagons up the incredible 1 in 27 gradient to Oldfield Road No.2 signal box, from where they would be collected by another locomotive. This involved setting back in the yard and taking a 'run' up the bank, a true display of raw steam power!   *Donald Cash*

62

Manchester Victoria to Oldham and Rochdale

The approach to Manchester Victoria station from the east is depicted in this photograph of Stanier Class 8F No.48557 descending the bank from Miles Platting with a coal train in tow. This picture was taken in March 1967. The tracks on the extreme right, which can just be seen, are the electrified lines to Bury which today form part of the city's tram system. The pair of tracks immediately to the right of the train serve Victoria station's terminal platforms which, at the time of this picture, were mainly used by local services to Oldham and stopping trains on the Huddersfield route. The line between Miles Platting and

Manchester Victoria, opened in 1844, was initially worked by a stationary engine hauling trains up the incline using a wire rope, a practice that lasted for two years, by which time steam engines were sufficiently powerful to ascend the 1 in 47/1 in 59 gradient without assistance. The line to Thorpes Bridge Junction via Cheetham Hill, which dated from 1877, curved away to the left behind the locomotive. Unfortunately, it is totally hidden from view by the coach on the left.   *Jim Davenport*

Photographed against the distinctive architecture of Lancashire mill buildings, an up evening parcels train, hauled by Class 5MT No.45290, passes Shaw on 19th June 1967. The photographer mentions that the mills still stand at the time of writing, and are now used as mail order warehouses, but the huge chimney, alas, has gone. The section of line between Oldham and Rochdale was built by the LYR, the company obtaining an Act in August 1859. The line opened for business on 1st December 1863.

Donald Cash

Right, above: The route between Oldham and Rochdale runs along the western fringe of the Pennine Chain, as evidenced by this shot of New Hey, with its exceedingly impressive and beautiful church perched atop the hill. The train is also worth a look! Judging by the massive load and the modest standards of this largely suburban line, it appears to be an excursion, probably heading for the traditional resorts of Blackpool or Southport. Let us hope it was not destined for a more distant destination, because the locomotive at the front end, Stanier Class 6P5F 'Jubilee' No.45623 *Palestine*, seems to be leaking a lot of steam, and was obviously not one of Newton Heath shed's best-maintained engines. Note the non-corridor compartment rolling stock, which was still employed on medium distance trains radiating from Manchester Victoria at that time. The absence of lavatory facilities in some of the coaches on the outward journey may have been an 'inconvenience', but the return trip was probably an ordeal for many passengers, particularly after a damp afternoon's drinking session in a sea-front pub! This illustration dates from 1963.

Richard Greenwood

Right, below: A busy scene at Rochdale with at least three steam locomotives in the station's environs in this portrait taken in 1962. The principal subject is 'Jubilee' 4-6-0 No.45717 *Dauntless* in charge of a trans-Pennine express, presumably from Leeds to Liverpool via Bradford Exchange: note the Gresley-designed coaches. An unidentified Class 5MT 4-6-0 waits at another platform, while a third steam engine, emitting a column of black smoke, is hidden from view. An excited young lad dashes along the platform to have a look at the 'Jubilee' before it departs. One wonders if he 'copped' it!

Donald Cash

Lees Motive Power Depot (Oldham)

Left, above: A portrait of a smartly turned-out Fowler-designed Class 4MT 2-6-4T No.42337 posing at Lees shed in April 1963. This locomotive was constructed at Derby Works in March 1929 and stayed in traffic at Stockport (Edgeley) shed for a further eight months after this shot was taken. Lees was a rather obscure shed, mainly providing locomotives for local freight work, on the former LNWR line from Oldham (Clegg Street) to Greenfield which lost its passenger service as early as 2nd May 1955. It was located adjacent to the former Lees station and consisted of a six-road dead-ended shed which was rebuilt in 1955. The shed was closed on 13th April 1964 and a housing estate now occupies the site. *Donald Cash*

Left, below: Aspinall-designed 0-6-0 No.52275, seen here sitting at the back of Lees shed, was one of no fewer than 448 of these locomotives built between 1889 and 1917. They were classified by the LYR as Class 27 and examples of the class were among the first superheated locomotives in Great Britain. The locomotives weighed 42tons 3cwt., had 5ft. 1in. driving wheels and possessed a tractive effort of 21,130lb. No.52275 was among the final survivors in service, being condemned in October 1962, the last representatives being withdrawn two months later. *Donald Cash*

The Facit Branch

The five miles-long branch from Rochdale to Facit was opened on 1st November 1870, and an extension was constructed to Bacup which started business on 1st December 1881. There were some fearsome gradients on this line, the final 3/4 mile-long section into Facit rising at 1 in 50. The stretch beyond there to Bacup climbed up to a summit at 967 feet above sea level between Britannia and Shawforth, so it must have been quite a line! Britannia station closed as long ago as 2nd April 1917, but the passenger service ran until 16th June 1947. This obscure route gained a higher profile in 1967 when the Locomotive Club of Great Britain and Roch Valley Railway Society

joined forces to operate a series of brake van trips using preserved LYR Class 0F 0-4-0ST No.51218. These dainty little engines were introduced in 1891 for use in sharply-curved sidings in docks and goods yards. This particular example first saw the light of day in 1901, being outshopped from Horwich Works as LYR No.68. In LYR days these locomotives worked at Fleetwood, Goole, Liverpool and Salford, but under BR could be found at such far-flung locations as Crewe, Swansea and York. Here, No.51218 creates a delightful image near Whitworth on 19th February 1967.   *Derek Huntriss*

The Bacup Branch

The beginnings of the Bacup branch can be traced back to 1844 when the Manchester, Bury & Rossendale Railway proposed a line to Rawtenstall which was to leave the Manchester to Bolton line at Clifton. The company obtained its Act on 4th July 1844, becoming part of the East Lancashire Railway on 21st July 1845: the route opened on 28th September 1846. A double track line was provided from Clifton Junction to Stubbins with a single track onwards to Rawtenstall, the latter being doubled at a later date. A link between Stubbins and Accrington, one of the most steeply graded routes in Lancashire, opened on 17th August 1848. On 27th March 1848 the Rawtenstall line was extended 1 3/4 miles to Newchurch. The ELR undertook a further extension, from Newchurch to Bacup, and the new line carried its first passengers on 1st October 1852: Bacup was on the railway map! The extension involved considerable heavy engineering work in a narrow gorge at Thrutch, where two single bore tunnels were driven through the hillside, the down line emerging into the open for a distance of 140 yards before plunging underground once again. The up line tunnel was continuous. Bacup stood at a higher elevation than any other town served by the ELR, the station being 800 feet above sea level. The railway had to contend with stiff road competition for much of its life initially from the Rossendale Valley Tramways (incorporated in 1888) which operated a service between Rawtenstall and Bacup. They employed steam trams through the streets until 1909. Road competition eventually proved to be the downfall of the Bacup line, which was cut back to Rawtenstall on 5th December 1966, and the entire route north of Bury was shut to passengers in 1972 – though the section between the last two named towns is back in use as part of the preserved East Lancashire Railway. Here, Ivatt 2-6-0 No.46437 and Stanier 2-6-4T No.42644 pose at Bacup with a 'last day' special on 3rd December 1966. *Jim Davenport*

Bolton Trinity Street Station

Right, above: An illustration of the eastern end of Bolton Trinity Street station taken from an overbridge on 20th April 1968. The train is a rail tour, one of many that criss-crossed the north west of England during the dying days of steam. Starting at Birmingham, the train visited Buxton, took the Standedge route over the Pennines, and also went over the Copy Pit line before reaching Bolton via Entwistle. Motive power included the inevitable Stanier 'Black Fives' and a Class 9F. The locomotives visible in this picture are BR Standard Class 5MT 4-6-0 Nos.73134, nearest to the camera, and 73069 which had worked the train from Stalybridge via Huddersfield, Hebden Bridge and Blackburn. The former is understood to have been the last of its class fitted with Caprotti valve gear still in traffic. The two locomotives are about to be replaced by Class 8F No.48773. *David Mitchell*

Right, below: In total contrast to the spacious layout at the eastern end of Bolton station, the western side of the premises was noted for its extremely tightly-curved triangular junction where the Blackburn line met the route from Preston. Note the proliferation of diamond crossings in this June 1965 photograph of the distinctive trackwork at this end of the station. Class 5MT No.45318 approaching with a short goods train almost seems to be of secondary interest! The course of the other curve here, which gave direct access to the Blackburn line from the Preston direction, can just be discerned on the right, in front of the buildings. Sadly, from the railway enthusiast's point of view, in recent years track components have been standardised as far as possible, thus robbing the system of much interest. *Brian Magilton*

The Horwich Branch

Left, above: Unlike other 'railway' towns, Horwich was thriving as a cotton finishing centre long before the railway came when the branch from (what later became) Blackrod was opened in February 1870. In this view, taken on a diabolically wet 19th September 1965, Stanier Class 4MT 2-6-4T No.42484 awaits departure with the 8.11am to Bolton. Latterly passenger services on the branch had been confined to peak hours only, principally for the benefit of works' employees. In the difficult economic situation of the early 1960s it was hardly surprising when the branch was tabled for closure, which occurred just over a week after this shot was taken.

Michael Allen

Left, below: The LYR's locomotive works at Horwich was opened on a green field site in 1887 replacing the cramped Miles Platting, Manchester, factory that was incapable of expansion. Following the transfer, the town's population increased from 4,000 to 12,850 in the five years from 1886. Nearly 2,000 locomotives were constructed at Horwich, the last being BR Standard Class 4MT No.76099 which was outshopped in 1957. Additionally, thousands of engines were overhauled there during the years, until repairs ceased in May 1964. Here, Aspinall-designed Class 2P 2-4-2T No.50647, which had been built at Horwich in 1890, rests outside the works in 1959, presumably awaiting cutting-up. Just in view is the front end of a LYR 0-6-0ST engine, five of which were kept as works' shunters for many years, curiously still bearing their LMSR numbers in the 113XX series.

G. Warnes/ Colour-Rail

A portrait of a lucky locomotive! No.49508 was one of 175 LMSR Standard Class 7F 0-8-0s built at Crewe Works in the years 1929-32. These engines were based on the LNWR G2 Class 0-8-0s, but were provided with smaller cylinders, higher working pressure, long travel valves and Walschaerts valve gear. Unfortunately, due to excessive zeal for standardisation at the time of their construction, they were also equipped with axleboxes the same size as those on the Class 4F 0-6-0s, and it was these undersized axleboxes which proved the Achilles' heel of the class. The locomotives were initially widely distributed, but were later concentrated on the Central Division at ex-LYR sheds. Due to their axlebox deficiencies the class was costly to maintain, and the engines also lacked vacuum brakes, this being another factor that probably hastened their downfall, so that by the end of 1951 only 53 were left in traffic. No.49508, seen here at Horwich Works following overhaul in June 1959, luckily survived this early holocaust and soldiered on to January 1962, when it was the last survivor.

P.J. Hughes/Colour-Rail

Finale

Stanier Class 8F 2-8-0 No.48348 exerts maximum effort, and emits a magnificent column of smoke, as it struggles to keep the 6.40pm Preston to Healey Mills freight train on the move on Farington curve, just south of Preston. This photograph was taken at around sunset on 9th April 1968.

Jeff Mimnagh